*Greater Than a T
Ebook and Audiob

Γ

n

Greater Than a Tourist Book Series
Reviews from Readers

I think the series is wonderful and beneficial for tourists to get information before visiting the city.

-Seckin Zumbul, Izmir Turkey

I am a world traveler who has read many trip guides but this one really made a difference for me. I would call it a heartfelt creation of a local guide expert instead of just a guide.

-Susy, Isla Holbox, Mexico

New to the area like me, this is a must have!

-Joe, Bloomington, USA

This is a good series that gets down to it when looking for things to do at your destination without having to read a novel for just a few ideas.

-Rachel, Monterey, USA

Good information to have to plan my trip to this destination.

-Pennie Farrell, Mexico

i

Great ideas for a port day.

-Mary Martin USA

Aptly titled, you won't just be a tourist after reading this book. You'll be greater than a tourist!

-Alan Warner, Grand Rapids, USA

Even though I only have three days to spend in San Miguel in an upcoming visit, I will use the author's suggestions to guide some of my time there. An easy read - with chapters named to guide me in directions I want to go.

-Robert Catapano, USA

Great insights from a local perspective! Useful information and a very good value!

-Sarah, USA

This series provides an in-depth experience through the eyes of a local. Reading these series will help you to travel the city in with confidence and it'll make your journey a unique one.

-Andrew Teoh, Ipoh, Malaysia

GREATER THAN A TOURIST- WYOMING USA

50 Travel Tips from a Local

Sara Rigsby

The statements in this book are of the authors and may not be the views of CZYK Publishing or Greater Than a Tourist.

First Edition

Cover designed by: Ivana Stamenkovic

Cover Image: https://pixabay.com/photos/wyoming-s-devils-tower-devils-tower-3915790/

Image 1: https://commons.wikimedia.org/wiki/File:Wyoming.JPG ErgoSum88 / Public domain

Image 2: https://commons.wikimedia.org/wiki/File:Barns_grand_tetons_mountains.jpg Jon Sullivan / Public domain

Image 3: https://commons.wikimedia.org/wiki/File:CheyenneWyoming.jpg Vasiliymeshko / CC BY-SA (https://creativecommons.org/licenses/by-sa/4.0)

Image 4: https://commons.wikimedia.org/wiki/File:EvanstonWyoming.jpg Vasiliymeshko / CC BY-SA (https://creativecommons.org/licenses/by-sa/4.0)

CZYK Publishing Since 2011.
Greater Than a Tourist

Lock Haven, PA
All rights reserved.

SBN: 9798649363006

>TOURIST

50 TRAVEL TIPS FROM A LOCAL

BOOK DESCRIPTION

With travel tips and culture in our guidebooks written by a local, it is never too late to visit Wyoming. Most travel books tell you how to travel like a tourist. Although there is nothing wrong with that, as part of the 'Greater Than a Tourist' series, this book will give you candid travel tips from someone who has lived at your next travel destination. This guide book will not tell you exact addresses or store hours but instead gives you knowledge that you may not find in other smaller print travel books. Experience cultural, culinary delights, and attractions with the guidance of a Local. Slow down and get to know the people with this invaluable guide. By the time you finish this book, you will be eager and prepared to discover new activities at your next travel destination.

Inside this travel guide book you will find:

  Visitor information from a Local
  Tour ideas and inspiration
  Save time with valuable guidebook information

Greater Than a Tourist- A Travel Guidebook with 50 Travel Tips from a Local. Slow down, stay in one place, and get to know the people and culture. By the time you finish this book, you will be eager and prepared to travel to your next destination.

OUR STORY

Traveling is a passion of the Greater than a Tourist book series creator. Lisa studied abroad in college, and for their honeymoon Lisa and her husband toured Europe. During her travels to Malta, an older man tried to give her some advice based on his own experience living on the island since he was a young boy. She was not sure if she should talk to the stranger but was interested in his advice. When traveling to some places she was wary to talk to locals because she was afraid that they weren't being genuine. Through her travels, Lisa learned how much locals had to share with tourists. Lisa created the Greater Than a Tourist book series to help connect people with locals. A topic that locals are very passionate about sharing.

TABLE OF CONTENTS

DEDICATION

This book is dedicated to the people of Wyoming. If I forgot something, please forgive me. Also to Scott, who was patient with me when I cooked hot dogs for dinner and neglected the dishes while writing this book.

ABOUT THE AUTHOR

Sara Rigsby has been calling Cheyenne, WY home for six years. She works for the State of Wyoming and spends her free time exploring the mountain west with her husband and two sons. She has lived in many places within the United States, and abroad as well. She views each new home as an opportunity to learn about culture, geography, and new ideas.

HOW TO USE THIS BOOK

The *Greater Than a Tourist* book series was written by someone who has lived in an area for over three months. The goal of this book is to help travelers either dream or experience different locations by providing opinions from a local. The author has made suggestions based on their own experiences. Please check before traveling to the area in case the suggested places are unavailable.

Travel Advisories: As a first step in planning any trip abroad, check the Travel Advisories for your intended destination.
https://travel.state.gov/content/travel/en/traveladvisories/traveladvisories.html

FROM THE PUBLISHER

Traveling can be one of the most important parts of a person's life. The anticipation and memories that you have are some of the best. As a publisher of the Greater Than a Tourist, as well as the popular *50 Things to Know* book series, we strive to help you learn about new places, spark your imagination, and inspire you. Wherever you are and whatever you do I wish you safe, fun, and inspiring travel.

Lisa Rusczyk Ed. D.
CZYK Publishing

WELCOME TO
> TOURIST

On Interstate 80, leaving Utah

Teton Range

City of Cheyenne, Wyoming

City of Evanston, Wyoming

"To travel is to live"

– Hans Christian Anderson

Wyoming is wild, wonderful, and growing. It is filled with outdoor adventure, western culture, and a laid back "work hard and play hard" attitude. There is luxury travel available in Wyoming, but most of the state is unpretentious, rustic, and open to all visitors willing to learn about Western history, ready to fearfully explore the mountains and parks, and interact cheerfully with its residents.

Wyoming has a unique history and culture. The State can boast the first woman to vote, the first woman governor, railroad expansion, and two spectacular National Parks. According to the Wyoming Office of Tourism, there are 100 species of mammals to spot in the state and 400 bird species. At least 48% of Wyoming is made up of public land that can be enjoyed by residents and visitors alike.

The largest city in Wyoming, Cheyenne, has 60,000 residents and it is trailed by Casper with approximately 57,500. The town of Buford famously has a population of 1. The small population and room to breathe are points of pride for Wyomingites who like solitude and wide-open spaces.

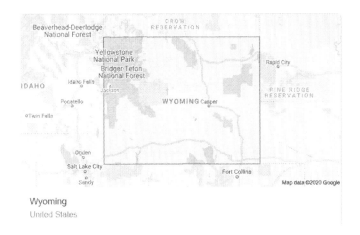

Wyoming
United States

Cheyenne Wyoming Climate

	High	Low
January	39	17
February	41	18
March	48	24
April	55	30
May	64	39
June	76	49
July	83	55
August	81	53
September	72	45
October	59	34
November	47	24
December	39	17

GreaterThanaTourist.com

Temperatures are in Fahrenheit degrees.
Source: NOAA

THE BASICS: WHAT YOU NEED TO KNOW BEFORE YOUR VISIT

1. THE BEST SITES IN WYOMING ARE ONLY ACCESSIBLE BY CAR (OR PICKUP TRUCK, OR CAMPER)

*"I take to the open road,
healthy, free, the world before me."*

– Walt Whitman

Wyoming is made up of wide-open spaces. Traveling throughout the state, and even in our towns and cities, is easiest in a personal vehicle. With a car, you will be able to access the most beautiful and remote sites, as well as the National Parks for limitless adventure.

If visiting in the winter, 4 wheel drive will be needed to navigate through the snow. When renting a vehicle in the summer, make sure that the vehicle has comprehensive insurance for unexpected weather events, particularly hail.

If renting a car or driving your own vehicle is not a possibility, there are several bus services in the state to get from city to city, including Greyhound and Express Arrow. Locally, there are rideshare apps like Uber and Lyft in some areas, but they are not as prevalent as they are in many bigger cities outside of Wyoming. The City of Cheyenne, Teton County, City of Casper, Sweetwater County, and Fremont County all have public bus systems. Make your travel plans ahead of time and expect delays when using these modes of transportation.

2. NEVER RUN ON EMPTY

Avoid getting stuck. When you see a gas station, stop for a fill-up, particularly if you are leaving a city for a long journey. There are gasoline deserts in Wyoming on I-25 and I-70 and on the back roads of Wyoming.

Do not plan on exploring Wyoming with an electric vehicle. Some of the cities are equipped with charging stations, but the infrastructure for a statewide road trip does not exist.

3. GETTING HERE

Wyoming may seem like a faraway land for some, but it is accessible to two major airports depending on what part of the state you plan to visit. Denver International Airport is about an hour and a half drive to Cheyenne and Salt Lake City International Airport is approximately a 4-hour drive to Jackson and an hour and a half drive to Evanston on I-80. There are regional airports in many of the towns in the state including Casper, Cheyenne, Cody, Jackson, Laramie, and Sheridan.

4. WINTER TRAVEL--YOUR FIRST WYOMING ADVENTURE

You came to Wyoming seeking adventure and excitement. Based on your "one death-defying adventure per trip" rule, driving on Wyoming's highways in the winter may make you reconsider the backcountry ski trip.

I-80 runs laterally across the state (well actually, all the way across the United States from Teaneck, NJ to San Francisco, CA) and it is driven by commuters, travelers, and truckers alike. I-80 in Wyoming on a day with wintry weather can be scary. On many days in the winter, I-80 is either fully or partially closed due to wind, snow, or ice. There are exceptions, and some days it does not close, despite the treacherous conditions. When driving I-80, be careful, slow down and drive in the right lane if the weather is questionable. Check with the Wyoming Department of Transportation's website before venturing out. There are parallel roads to drive as a detour, but they often close in the winter when the highways are closed.

In addition to I-80, there are warnings or closures for wind on I-25 between Cheyenne and Casper as well. If you are towing a camper or trailer, pay close attention to the warnings for high profile vehicles. I have seen many turned over on their sides on I-25 and I-80. Be prepared to be flexible with your plans.

Warning: There are big fines for driving through barriers on closed roads. Instead, stay put until the weather improves.

5. HYDRATION IN HIGH ELEVATION

Bring a water bottle and stay hydrated. Wyoming is second to Colorado in altitude in the United States with a mean elevation of 6,700 feet. According to the Institute for Altitude Medicine, even the healthiest of people may have difficulty adjusting to higher altitudes and can develop a hangover like headache. Other symptoms may include vomiting, difficulty sleeping, dizziness, and weakness. When making the adjustment to a higher elevation the Institute recommends an extra liter or 1.5 liters of water. Some other tips to adjust to higher altitude from the Institute--avoid alcohol and excessive exercise for a day or two.

6. GIVE THE ANIMALS SOME SPACE

Each year we hear about a poor soul getting too close to a wild animal resulting in serious injury or death. The animals in State and National Parks are familiar with people and therefore may seem docile, but they are still wild and can be dangerous. The Yellowstone National Park website suggests:

Stay least 100 yards from bears and wolves (the length of a soccer field) and 25 yards away from other animals like elk and bison (the length of an Olympic size swimming pool).

Keep on marked trails and paths

Never feed the animals or leave uneaten food behind

Stay in your vehicle if you encounter wildlife in the road

7. KNOW YOUR BEARS

Black bears live throughout the state and grizzly bears can be found in the western part of the state. How do you tell the difference? A black bear has pointed ears, a straight face profile, and short claws. A grizzly bear is most recognized by the hump on its shoulder. It has short round ears and a scooped face profile. They are absolutely beautiful and even look a little cuddly, but bears need to be admired from a distance because they can be dangerous. Grizzly bears are more aggressive than black bears, nevertheless, it is important to keep a distance from all bears.

8. GET BEAR SPRAY

Bear Spray is necessary for hiking and camping in many parts of Wyoming in the unlikely possibility that you may encounter an aggressive bear. It is available at most outdoor stores and many big box stores. Bear spray is similar to pepper spray, the chemical that many people keep on hand for protection from other people, but it has a different concentration of the ingredients, therefore, it should only be used on bears. It can reach 1.5 to 3 meters depending on the brand. Use as it is directed. In some areas of the county, bear spray is illegal to use, but it is encouraged in Wyoming and the state's National Parks. The safest way to protect yourself from a bear, though, is to keep your distance.

9. CAN YOU HEAR ME NOW? MOBILE PHONE SERVICE

"There is no wifi in the forest, but I promise you will find a better connection."

-Anonymous

Although it is improving every day, mobile phone coverage can be unreliable in the middle of the state and even along I-80 from Rawlins to Evanston. Mobile phone coverage is available in 50% of Yellowstone National Park and in most of Grand Teton National Park, thanks to its proximity to Jackson Hole. Many of the State Parks do not have mobile phone coverage. Be prepared to unplug for much of your visit.

10. WINTER, SUMMER REPEAT--BE PREPARED FOR TWO SEASONS, ALL YEAR ROUND

"This… is Berk. It snows nine months of the year… and hails the other three."

-From the movie "How to Train Your Dragon"

Weather in Wyoming can be unpredictable. The summers will bring the best weather you will ever experience, with low humidity and mild temperatures. On the other hand, in the late afternoons of summer, you may find yourself dodging hail, sometimes as big as golf balls.

Snow can begin in late September and almost always falls into May. There is gusty wind nearly every day in the winter. Mixed in with these wintry days are also spring-like days in the 50s and 60s in January and February.

With the exception of those visiting for skiing or hunting, most tourists visit Wyoming in June, July, and August. Temperatures can drop down to the 40s at night, with 80-degree afternoons. In order to witness starry skies at night and elk bugling at dawn, bring layers and hats and gloves, even in the summer. Experiencing Wyoming means spending a significant amount of time outside. Being comfortable in all weather will make the visit all the more pleasurable.

A pair of hiking pants that can roll up or zip off into shorts are useful for Wyoming travel in the summer. Also, a lightweight fleece jacket to get you through the chilly mornings and evenings.

11. HIKING BOOTS CAN GET YOU A LONG WAY

"Give a girl the right shoes and she can conquer the world"

-Marilyn Monroe (This applies to men too, of course).

Find a pair of sturdy, comfortable hiking boots or hiking shoes. Plenty of people have hiked some of Wyoming's scenic trails in tennis shoes, but a pair of comfortable hiking boots or hiking shoes will provide steadier footing on rough terrain. It is best to buy hiking boots or shoes from a reputable store with experienced sales personnel, rather than online. Do some research on the type of boot you will need based on the terrain, length of your trip, the expected weather, and how much weight you will carry. Lightweight hiking shoes are perfect for short hikes and as everyday wear while traveling. Many people prefer a sturdy boot for day-long or overnight trips.

Get some mileage in your new shoes before traveling. Break them in at the grocery store, strolling through the neighborhood and short hikes near home.

12. LEAVE IT AS YOU FOUND IT

I have seen visitors with out of state license plates take a large rock from a National Forest in Wyoming, and place it in their vehicle, presumably to decorate their home garden. The rock was so large that two people had to carry it. Wyoming has beautiful rocks, plants, and timber and it is tempting to take a piece of nature home as a free souvenir. At the risk of sounding like your mother, if everyone did that there would be nothing left. Please avoid the temptation to take items from the natural scene while you are exploring. Take photos instead!

When picnicking, camping, or hiking, take all the items you brought either back with you or disposed of in the proper trash receptacles. Avoid leaving garbage or any other personal artifacts in the National Forest, State Parks or National Parks. It's helpful to bring along a few bags designated as garbage bags in your luggage or vehicle. The bears, bison, and black-billed cuckoos will thank you. So will the other visitors.

FOOD AND DRINK
13. THE LOCAL FIREWATER

*"I need the anesthetic qualities
of the local firewater."*

- Anthony Bourdain from "Parts Unknown
(Colombia)"

Rounding off a day of adventure with a locally produced beverage can be relaxing. Wyoming has enough breweries and distilleries to keep your evenings busy.

14. DISTILLERIES

The Backwards Distillery in Casper, WY is an old-timey circus-themed distillery producing vodka, rum, and gin promised to have a little twist of the unusual.

Located in the Big Horn Mountains, Wyoming Whiskey in Kirby, WY, is a distillery owned and operated by a prominent family in Wyoming, the Meads. The distillery touts itself as producing America's Best Craft Whiskey.

In Pine Bluffs, WY, almost in Nebraska in the Southeastern corner of the state, Pine Bluffs Distilling is a newer business making whiskey, bourbon, and vodka from local ingredients.

Finally, Jackson Hole Still Works also produces its whiskey, vodka, and gin from local ingredients.

Most of the distilleries in Wyoming use locally sourced ingredients to produce purely Wyoming liquors. All of the distilleries mentioned are open for tours and tastings. Most of these liquors are sold at local liquor stores as well.

15. BREWERIES

The brewing industry is budding in Wyoming and at least one brewery can be found in almost every city.

In Cheyenne, Accomplice Beer Company in the Depot, has a self pour set up where customers can pour the brewery's seven signature beers. The menu is small, but the food is delicious. We bring our children and they enjoy watching the trains go by while we drink our beer and kale salad.

The Melvin Brewery, with tasting rooms in Jackson and Alpine, is considered by many as the best brewery in Wyoming and was the Great American Beer Festival Winner for best beer group in 2017. This brewery is

29

popular and growing. Taste it now so you can claim you "knew it before it was big."

Blacktooth brewery in Sheridan is a well established and popular brewery in the state with three flagship beers and several seasonal options with the catchy slogan "Drink the West."

16. WINERIES

Wyoming's rough and dry terrain is not known for producing wine, but there are several wineries throughout the state including Table Mountain Vineyards in Torrington and Jackson Hole Winery.

17. MOVE OVER VEGETARIANS

Wyoming is a great place for meat-eaters to visit. Cattle is the largest agricultural industry in the state. From the comfort of your home anywhere in the United States, you can order a portion of a Wyoming cow and have it shipped to your home from Wyoming Pure Natural Beef. Many Wyoming families will split a cow amongst each other or order from a local company for the best beef.

Bison is also on the menu at many restaurants in Wyoming, it is leaner beef-like meat and is often served in the form of a burger. You can also find elk steak and burgers on menus in Wyoming. This is lean red meat with a mild taste. My family eats elk as a replacement for beef in most recipes.

If you dare, also try rocky mountain oyster (the testicles of a bull, pig, or sheep). They are often served fried with a lot of breading so you don't dwell much on what you are eating.

Vegetarians, there is a very popular vegetarian restaurant in Laramie called Sweet Melissa. There is a place for you in Wyoming too!

THREE CITIES AND A RESERVATION

There are more than three cities in Wyoming, but only one reservation. These are four recommended go-to stops while traveling in the state.

18. IF YOU ONLY HAVE TIME FOR ONE DESTINATION IN WYOMING VISIT SHERIDAN

My favorite city in Wyoming is Sheridan. Just north of the Big Horn Mountains close to the Montana state line, Sheridan is a small city with sophistication, beauty, and history. Sheridan has a small downtown with restaurants, a wine bar, boutiques, and art, with a stunning backdrop of valleys and mountains. Sheridan hosts events throughout the year in its downtown and also in the nearby mountains. If you chose to spend a few days in Wyoming, Sheridan would be the best choice for a base to explore the nature of Wyoming in the Big Horn Mountains while spending time in a delightful small city. Sheridan has a small airport for quick access to Denver International Airport.

19. JACKSON HOLE: WESTERN WEALTH AND WILDERNESS

Jackson Hole is one of the wealthiest communities in the country and also a wonderful place to visit. The area is south of Grand Teton National Park and is home to world-class skiing, remarkable restaurants, and the famous arch in its town square constructed of elk antlers. Jackson Hole preserves the old west culture of Wyoming with a little bit of luxury. The accommodations in Jackson Hole can range from affordable to extravagant so there is something for every visitor. Jackson Hole is bustling all year round with summer and winter activities to enjoy, stunning scenery, and frequent community events happily mixing tourists with locals.

20. LIVE THE LEGEND IN CHEYENNE

Cheyenne is the Capital of Wyoming and offers an abundance of free activities for families looking for fun and learning. The Capitol Building is open to the public most days of the year so visitors can learn about Wyoming's history and the politics of the state. The Botanic Gardens with an attached Children's Village is an amazing free activity for families. The Children's Village highlights sustainable energy sources with interactive exhibits and frequent organized children's activities. The Wyoming State Museum, also free, has interactive exhibits on wildlife, Native Americans, fossils, and the mining industry.

Downtown Cheyenne, like many downtowns in the United States, is going through a renaissance. Find free live music at the Cheyenne Depot on Fridays in the summer, boutique shopping, and delicious restaurants like Bella Fuoco for pizza, or Rib and Chop House for a heartier steak dinner. There are several breweries downtown. Each July, Cheyenne is host to Cheyenne Frontier Days, the largest outdoor rodeo in the country.

Need some retail therapy? Downtown Cheyenne has several antique shops, a Wyoming themed home furnishings store, and other shops worth a look. Also, Cheyenne is home to Sierra Trading Post, the classic casual and outdoor wear company. The flagship store is on Campstool Road south of downtown.

21. WIND RIVER RESERVATION

Wind River Reservation is located south of the Shoshone National Forest and east of the southern portion of Bridget-Teton National Forest in the Wind River Basin. It is a 2.2 million-acre reservation that belongs to the Eastern Shoshone and the Northern

Arapaho Tribes. There are 240 lakes on the reservation and the stunning Wind River Canyon. Visitors are welcome on the reservation and encouraged to take time to learn about the people living there. There are several online driving tours of the reservation which may teach you a few things and help you navigate the immense acreage.

22. THINGS TO DO ON THE RESERVATION:

The Northern Arapaho Experience Room in the Wind River Hotel and Casino has displays of art, artifacts, historical information, and dance exhibitions every Tuesdays.

Visit the Wind River Wild Horse Sanctuary, one of three horse sanctuaries in Wyoming. Visitors can learn about the importance of horses in Native American culture, take an ATV tour of the sanctuary, go horseback riding or arrange a wild horse adoption

Attend a powwow. Both tribes host powwows in the summer months. These events are celebrations of cultural heritage with prayer, dancing, and singing. Visitors are welcome, but to honor your hosts, please review etiquette information before attending.

The Eastern Shoshone and Northern Arapaho tribes are very different in culture and tradition. Be sure to respect each tribe as a separate entity and learn about how they live and waork together on the same reservation.

TIME TO EXPLORE: THINGS TO DO

23. HIKE YOUR HEART OUT

"In every walk with nature one receives more than he seeks."

-John Meir

Hiking provides travelers with exercise, an opportunity to spot wildlife, and the ability to experience views that people popping in and out of their vehicles may never see. When selecting a hike, look at the length of the hike and the elevation of the hike to assess its difficulty.

Escape the crowds in Teton National Park and Yellowstone National Park by finding one of the hundreds of trails to trek. Favorite trails include 7-

mile circle Jenny Lake Trail in Teton National Park and 7 miles, out and back, Mount Washburn in Yellowstone National Park. The park rangers are invaluable resources for identifying hikes and points of interest.

Other fabulous hikes around the state include 10 miles, out and back, Laramie Peak in Garret, WY. The Snowy Mountains, west of Laramie, WY have an abundance of short and accessible hikes with stunning views, and also a more challenging hike up 3.4-mile hike up 12,018 to Medicine Bow Peak.

Cloud Peak Wilderness and Big Horn National Forest near Sheridan, WY have 1,200 miles worth of trails and something for every ability level.

Gannett Peak, part of the Wind River Range in Fremont County, is the highest peak in Wyoming at 13,810 feet. It is difficult to ascend, with some icy patches that will require special equipment. Guides are available for hire to help navigate this challenging hike.

24. NATIONAL PARK ADVENTURES

"There is nothing so American as our national parks... The fundamental idea behind the parks...is that the country belongs to the people, that it is in process of making for the enrichment of the lives of all of us."

- President Franklin D. Roosevelt

Teton National Park and Yellowstone National Park are both spectacular in beauty and are overflowing with exciting experiences. Both parks make up much of the western part of the state and are connected. Grand Teton National Park is in the south and Yellowstone National Park to the north. Grand Teton National Park is an abundant wilderness of gorgeous mountains and lakes. This park provides visitors with natural beauty, great wildlife sitings, and opportunities to enjoy the natural wild west. For a deeper look into volcanic activity, getting up close and personal with the bison, and a geyser you can set your clock to, visit Yellowstone National Park.

Both parks are very popular, but Yellowstone seems to have more vehicle traffic and Grand Teton National Park has more outdoor exploration. Some hints for visiting these parks:

Attend a ranger talk. These evening events are available to lodgers, campers, and people willing to stay in the park late enough to hear the stories and lessons from the experts under the stars.

Don't be afraid to get out of your vehicle and explore a little. These parks are enormous and there is a lot to explore off the beaten path. Track down a park ranger for suggestions. Park rangers are experts on the parks and can provide suggestions not available on the internet or in books.

Carry water and snacks. Although there are stops throughout the parks, be prepared in case you are not able to make it to a shop or restaurant as soon as expected.

Fill up before entering the park. You will need gas to get around, especially Yellowstone, so be sure to be prepared with a full tank of gas. There are gas stations in the parks, but entering the park with a full tank is a good practice.

Book a room ahead of time. Visitors planning on lodging in one of the National Parks should plan on booking a room a year or more in advance.

Sometimes there are last-minute cancellations, so if you are flexible you may be able to grab a room with seconds to spare. My family has benefited from cancellations several times, but it is definitely not a certainty. Back-up plans for lodging are a good idea.

Book dinner at the Moran Room in Jackson Lake Lodge at Grand Teton National Park. Enjoy the best view in the world while dining on fine food.

25. WYOMING STATE PARKS

There's a joke in Wyoming that it is spring when the license plates turn green. People from Colorado come, with their green license plates, to enjoy Wyoming's less crowded and stunning State Parks for recreation. Most State Parks offer fishing, trails, and camping. There are 13 state parks in Wyoming with unique features to each.

State Park highlights include:

A huge lake, with boat rentals, at Glendo State Park

Well-known and extensive mountain bike trails at Curt Gowdy State Park.

Treehouse accommodations at Keyhole State Park.

Tip: Before heading to the State Park research fees and bring exact change or a check. The State Parks do not take debit or credit cards at this time.

26. CHEYENNE FRONTIER DAYS

Grab your boots and hat, and join the community of Cheyenne at the world's largest outdoor rodeo. Each July, the rodeo community has its eyes on Cheyenne Frontier Days. More than 90,000 people visit the Professional Rodeo Cowboys Association competitive rodeo events such as barrel racing, steer wrestling and bull riding and approximately 120,000 attend the evening concerts featuring the latest country acts, the occasional pop performance and a few classic bands as well. The rodeo also hosts an Indian Village with authentic Native education and entertainment. There are booths upon booths of western knick-knacks and a carnival. The small city of Cheyenne is turned upside down for 2 weeks each year.

In addition, there are parades every other morning in downtown Cheyenne showcasing carriages from

the early days of Cheyenne with local residents
dressed in period costumes. On alternate mornings is
a pancake breakfast. The Kiwanis Club and the Boy
Scouts flip over 100,000 pancakes for locals and
visitors at this free event.

27. FISHING, THE GREAT WESTERN PASTIME

Wyoming is known for its fishing. There's ice
fishing, fly fishing, and lakeside fishing. Fishing is a
favorite pastime of locals and draws thousands of
tourists. The Wyoming Game and Fish Department is
the best resource for information on fishing licenses,
fishing locations, and rules and regulations. The
department has a website and is also active on social
media. There are also fly fishing guides available to
help visitors have the best experience.

28. RELAX IN THE HOT SPRINGS

Enjoy a dip in a hot springs pool on a chilly
Wyoming night (or day). Since Wyoming evenings

have a bit of chill in all seasons, visiting hot springs is a year-round event that is relaxing and therapeutic.

At Saratoga Resort and Spa, in Saratoga, you will step outside of your room into a courtyard of private hot spring pools. It is the ultimate convenience, especially in frigid weather. The resort also has a brewery and restaurant along with a spa. Like most of Wyoming, the resort is unpretentious, welcoming, and truly enjoyable.

Hot spring swimming holes can also be found in Hot Springs State Park in Thermopolis, Granite Hot Springs in Jackson, and the Hobo Pool in Saratoga. Most hot springs in the United States require swimwear, so do not forget to drop into a store and pick up a bathing suit if you did not pack one.

Warning: Many hot springs are too hot for swimming. Only swim in designated hot springs pools.

29. ROCK FORMATIONS

In Wyoming, you will find outstanding rock formations. It is a paradise for rock climbers, geology hobbyists, or tourists with an eye for unique natural beauty. The most famous rock formation in Wyoming is Devils Tower National Monument in Crook County, nestled in the Northeast corner of the state. Devil's tower is 867 feet tall and is made of phonolite porphyry, meaning it was formed from magma that condensed into columns. This site is a sacred site for Northern Plains Indians and is visited by many tourists a year to awe in its beauty and for experienced climbers to ascend. If you plan to climb the Tower, visit the National Parks website for rules and regulations.

Vedawoo, pronounced Ve-dah-voo, is a section of Medicine Bow-Routt National Forest located outside of Cheyenne. It is a garden of Sherman granite outcroppings, that, according to the National Forest Service, were thought by Native Americans to be stacked by playful spirits. It has also served as a hideout for famous Western outlaws. Today, Vedauwoo is a natural playground and campsite for Cheyenne residents and visitors. Rock climbing can be enjoyed by children and experts alike.

Castle Gardens Petroglyphs Site, near Riverton, WY is the site of explorable rock formations and

Native American rock art or Petroglyphs. According to the Bureau of Land Management (BLM), gravel paths have been built throughout the site, along with footbridges to make the site more accessible to visitors. The BLM does warn that to access the site you may want to drive a high profile 4 wheel drive vehicle like a truck or an SUV.

Some other rock formations in Wyoming worth checking out are Castle Rock in Green River, Hell's Half Acre in Natrona County and Pilot Butte near Rock Springs.

Ski, Snowshoe or Snowmobile Through a Winter Wonderland
Most people visit Wyoming in the summer, but there are amazing winter activities to experience like snowshoeing, skiing, and snowmobiling.

The western side of the state is best known for its alpine, or downhill, skiing in Jackson Hole and Cokeville. There are also ski areas outside of Casper and Laramie that are affordable, less crowded, and great for beginner skiers.

Snowshoeing, Nordic (or cross-country) skiing, and snowmobiling activities are available in every corner of the state with rentals readily accessible. Winter can be bitterly cold, but also sunny and beautiful. Be sure to dress appropriately with layers and warm accessories.

The best of the best winter activities:

Snowshoe: Wyomingites recommend the Darby Canyon Wind Trail in Alta. It is a 6.9-mile trail with the reward of a waterfall view.

Snowmobile: Snowmobile in a deserted Yellowstone National Park. With a guide, see Old Faithful with a winter backdrop and without the crowds. Reservations are recommended.

Nordic Skiing: Beaver Creek Nordic Ski Area in Lander has groomed trails and organized events for nordic ski enthusiasts.

Warning: Most years there is a story in the news about a family getting lost while snowmobiling in Wyoming. Hiring a guide is a safe and recommended practice for visitors unfamiliar with the area. If that is not possible, bring a GPS.

30. GOING ON A DINOSAUR HUNT

Wyoming has an extensive paleontological history and there are several exciting sites to learn about the dinosaurs that once roamed the land in Wyoming. The first stop on your dinosaur tour must be the Wyoming Dinosaur Center and Dig Sites in Thermopolis. This was named one of the World's Coolest Places for Kids by Time Magazine. It is an enormous museum of dinosaur fossils and information about the giants that once roamed Earth. Sign up to tour the nearby dinosaur dig site and even excavate some bones yourself. This is a modern, unique natural history museum dedicated entirely to dinosaurs.

The Tate Geological Museum in Casper has the bones of a tyrannosaurus rex and the bones of one of the largest mammoths ever found. In addition, visitors can sign up for a week of excavation finding fossils at active dig sites.

The Paleon Museum in Glenrock is a large museum and also hosts day digs, 2-day digs, and week-long digs to bring out your inner paleontologist.

31. WILD WEST RANCHER

Do you dream of staying on a ranch, wrangling cows, and riding horses into the wild blue yonder? Wyoming has a dude ranch adventure for every style and pocketbook.

Eatons Ranch is the oldest guest ranch in Wyoming. It is located in Wolf, WY near the Big Horn Mountains. There are activities for families, children's programs, fishing, swimming, overnight horseback trips, and exercise classes.

The Vee Bar Guest Ranch in Laramie, WY has rave reviews as a family-oriented western adventure and is favored by locals. Families can enjoy horseback riding, evening campfires, trap shooting, and cattle herding.

Wyoming is also home to luxury dude ranches that pamper visitors enjoying the wild west. Outside Saratoga is the Brush Creek Ranch that hosts celebrity and wealthy families on the same adventures as the other ranches, but with upscale accommodations including "glamping" and spa services.

32. COUNTY FAIRS AND THE STATE FAIR

In the summer county fairs and the Wyoming State Fair in Douglas are a great way to spend a day or evening celebrating the local culture. The fairs have youth livestock shows, tractor pulls, Mutton Bustin' (think small children as young as 5 "bull riding" on sheep), agricultural competitions, rodeo events, and outdoor concerts. Most county fairs have a carnival component with rides, games, and fried food. It is an ideal way to connect with the local community and experience something new.

33. UNIVERSITY OF WYOMING

The University of Wyoming is the only four-year college and graduate school in Wyoming. It sits in Laramie, WY, and is the lifeblood of that unique community. The University's catchphrase is "The world needs more cowboys." The University has an art museum that is free to visitors and boasts traveling exhibits, student and teacher exhibits, and community learning opportunities. The University of Wyoming Geological Museum, also free to the public, has a wide array of dinosaur fossils found in Wyoming for learning and exploration.

Wyoming sports fans are a hearty bunch and will attend a University of Wyoming Cowboys football game in freezing temperatures with raging winds. There are tickets available for all of the university's sports teams such as basketball, soccer and, of course, football. Witness the dedicated fans and Cowboy spirit of the state's only university.

While in Laramie, eat at Anong's Thai Cuisine and visit the unique shops and boutiques downtown.

34. BROWSE THE BOOKSTORES

"What I say is, a town isn't a town without a bookstore. It may call itself a town, but unless it's got a bookstore, it knows it's not foolin' a soul."

-Neil Gaiman

Take a break from the road and peruse a local bookstore and have a cup of coffee. Most towns in

Wyoming have an independent bookstore where you can explore local authors and in many, take a coffee break for more than just a shopping experience. In Thermopolis, Storyteller has a large general and local selection of books and a coffee shop (they roast their own coffee too). Wandering Hermit Books in Wheatland sells bestsellers, children's books, and local gifts. Sit down with a book, a cup of tea, and enjoy the cozy fireplace. Downtown Rock Springs' Sidekick's Book and Wine Bar has a large variety of books from children's books to cookbooks and also sells wine, appetizers, and desert mixing a social atmosphere with a love of reading.

35. ANTLER HUNT

Every spring in March and April, bull (male) elk shed their antlers. Starting in May locals and many people from surrounding states become shed hunters wandering through elk country looking to acquire an antler. If you see an antler on the ground and are in the antler hunting area (see Wyoming Game and Fish's website for the map) between May and December, feel free to pick it up and take it home. Most people use the antlers for home decoration like chandeliers, yard ornaments, picture frames, candleholders, and fruit baskets.

Tip: If the antler is attached to an elk skull it is not a shed. You will need to contact the Wyoming Game and Fish Department and pay a fee to remove it from the site.

TRAVEL BACK IN TIME

36. RAILROADING THROUGH HISTORY

"The introduction of so powerful
an agent as steam to a carriage on
wheels will make a great change in
the situation of man."

— Thomas Jefferson, 1802

According to the Wyoming Office of Tourism, the Union Pacific Railroad first came to Cheyenne in 1867. Since then, the railroad has served as an influential part of the Wyoming economy and culture.

Wyoming is a great place to explore the Transcontinental Railroad. Learn about the railroad history of Cheyenne and the building of the transcontinental railroad at the Cheyenne Depot Museum and Museum Shop. Also in Cheyenne, is a Big Boy 4004 steam engine in Holliday Park and Ol' Sadie, engine 1242 in Lion's Park. Ol' Sadie is surrounded by a fence constructed by its last conductor. The fence is made of steel artifacts found along the tracks across the State. It is an interesting piece of art in itself.

In Laramie, the Laramie Railroad Depot provides an interactive exhibit about the history of trains in the State. In the adjacent Railroad Heritage Park you will find a unique snow plow train car, an engine, a bunk car, and a caboose.

In Rawlins, there is another Depot seeped in Wyoming railroad history. This building has been transformed into a community center but is open to the public for viewing. The railroad also went through the towns of Rock Springs and Evanston. Rock Springs has a history museum with information on its railroad roots. In Evanston, you can grab a brochure or download a walking tour of the town's Roundhouse and Railyard.

37. THE OLD WEST

Wyoming is seeping with Western History. There are several sites not to miss. Starting in Cheyenne, learn about many details about the state's history with the Cheyenne Trolley Tour. The tour starts at the Cheyenne Depot and drives through downtown sharing nuggets of historical information about the capital city and the state.

In Laramie, visit the Wyoming Territorial Prison Historic Site that housed some of the West's most notorious outlaws, including Butch Cassidy. Learn about the prison, the history, and those who put the "wild" in the Wild West. Also in Southeast Wyoming is Ft. Laramie. Ft. Laramie, which is managed by the National Park Service, was a fur trading post and then later an influential military outpost. Active for 56 years, this site holds stories of expansion, the United States' relationship with Native Americans, and even the Pony Express. Tour the grounds to learn the stories of a base essential for the survival of settlers moving west.

The Grand Encampment Museum, located in Carbon County, has the acclaim of a much larger museum in a much larger city. This well-received and reviewed museum features the history of the local area with over a dozen historical buildings and information on the industries of mining, timber, and agriculture. The collection of artifacts is one of a kind, making this a fun learning opportunity.

In Cody, the Buffalo Bill Museum of the West will leave you in awe and appreciation of western culture. This large, state of the art facility houses 5 museums in one: Buffalo Bill Museum, Plains Indian Museum, Whitney Western Art Museum, Draper Natural History Museum, and the Cody Firearms Museum.

Rock Springs is known for its exciting history. On the railroad route in Wyoming, this city has a history of recruiting international immigrants to work. Driving through town you will see 56 flags honoring the cultural heritage of its residents. Rock Springs also has a historical museum covering its relationship with the railroad, its mining history, and its famous outlaw residents.

38. THE EQUALITY STATE

Named the Equality State, Wyoming was the first state to allow women to vote and also had the first woman governor in the country, Nellie Tayloe Ross. In Laramie, visit the Wyoming House for Historic Women and the American Heritage Center at the University of Wyoming for a look into women's history in the state. In addition, visit South Pass City and learn about William Bright, the Wyoming legislator, who first introduced the women's suffrage bill and also the location of the first appointed woman official, Ester Hobart Morris, the town's justice of the peace. On the Wind River Reservation, visit Sacajawea's gravesite to honor the woman who assisted Lewis and Clark on their expedition from North Dakota to the Pacific Ocean.

39. COLD WAR MISSILES

If the United States Cold War history piques your interest, you probably know that the great plains played, and still plays, a crucial role in housing nuclear missiles. The State of Wyoming has taken over the Quebec 01 Missile Site and has restored it to its original condition (minus the missile) and opened it to the public. Visitors will see how the site appeared to the missileers, get an overview of Cold War History, and learn about the deactivation of the system. The site is 30 minutes north of Cheyenne and there is a nominal entry fee.

40. JAY EM, GHOST TOWN

Jay Em is Wyoming's ghost town. Located in Goshen County, Jay Em had a bank, a repair shop, a gas station, and a general store and served as a hub for local ranchers. As the use of the automobile spread, so did its residents and it became deserted in the late 1930s. You can still see the buildings of this deserted town and imagine what it looked like as a small, but essential commerce hub for settlers in pre-vehicle Wyoming.

41. TEAPOT DOME

The Teapot Dome Scandal is one of the most significant incidents of political corruption in United States history and it happened under Warren G. Harding's White House. The scandal, in short, led to bribery, a murder-suicide, and the incarceration of the US Secretary of the Interior. This famous scandal was named for one of the oil fields involved, Teapot Dome about 30 miles north of Casper. The actual oil field is not open to visitors, but tourists can view Teapot Rock, the rock formation which the oil field and, in turn, the scandal were named for. The rock no longer looks like a teapot due to erosion but is still an eye-catching rock formation to check out if your travels take you to the Casper area.

ONLY IN WYOMING

42. THE JACKALOPE: WYOMING'S OFFICIAL MYTHICAL CREATURE

The Jackalope may be a mythical creature, but it is alive and well in Wyoming. The Jackalope, invented by a team of taxidermist brothers in Douglas is the hybrid of a jackrabbit and a deer (not an antelope as some may assume by its moniker). Douglas is considered the "Jackalope Capital of the World." The creature is honored with several statues including an 8-foot-tall jackalope and a newer larger 13-foot version. The City of Douglas issues hunting licenses for Jackalope. Hunting Jackalope is only permitted on the 31st of June between midnight and 2 am. 250 miles down the road the City of Dubois claims to have the world's largest stuffed Jackalope at the Country Store. The State of Wyoming made the Jackalope its official mythical creature in 2005.

43. MEET A COWBOY...OR AT LEAST SOMEONE WHO LOOKS LIKE A COWBOY

"Boots, chaps, and cowboy hats.
Nothing else matters."

-Anonymous

Most people in Wyoming wear normal casual streetwear, but you may come across a person or two, especially during the summer's rodeo season, dressed in Western wear. Western wear may include a cowboy hat, boots, jeans, and snap-button shirts. Also, large belt buckles, bolo ties, and calf-length skirts. People in Wyoming love their western roots and most residents own a western outfit or two for special themed occasions. Some Wyomingites dress in western fashion 365 days of the year.

If you are interested in updating your wardrobe with some studded jeans and boots, there is plenty of shopping throughout the state. For western shopping, experiences visit The Wrangler in downtown Cheyenne, Martindales Western Shop in Laramie, Custom Cowboy Shop in Cody, and Lou Taubert Ranch Outfitters in Casper. Locals save a little money and shop at the Boot Barn and Murdochs, both chains with locations throughout the state.

Here's a tip: If you are in the market for a hat, consider the season. In the summer cowboys and cowgirls wear white hats to keep them cool. They sport dark hats in the winter months to attract the sun and keep warm.

44. UNIQUELY WYOMING

There are some man-made spots that are "uniquely Wyoming" and need to be pointed out. In Story, WY, a small town south of the Big Horn Mountains is the most unique house I've stayed at in my travels: the Waldorf A'Story Guest Haus. Far from the Waldorf Astoria luxury hotels, the home is filled with kitschy trinkets, barstools carved from tree trunks, an outdoor fire pit, a picnic table by a bubbling creek to enjoy a meal and even a framed letter from the Waldorf Astoria threatening legal action of the use of the name. This guest house has secrets and surprises around every corner making the stay anything but dull.

The Bunkhouse Bar and Grill is a restaurant and saloon west of Cheyenne on Happy Jack Road. Join the locals in country swing dancing on Friday and Saturday night, steak dinners, and a true Wyoming cowboy decor. Some patrons ride their horses and tie them up in front to drink the night away. Before you decide to ride your horse to the bar in Wyoming, although it is not possible to get arrested for driving under the influence while riding a horse, there are other citations, like public drunkenness, that may be issued.

61

In Grand Teton National Park, travel to Mormon Row and find what might be the most photographed barn in America. The T.A. Moulton Barn is listed in the National Register of Historic Places and can be found on far and wide on social media using hashtag #MoultonBarn. The barn is a unique shape and the setting is beyond picturesque providing the perfect photo-sharing opportunity.

45. FIREARMS IN PUBLIC

"The right of the citizens to bear arms in defense of themselves and the state shall not be denied."

State Constitutional Provision - Article 1, Section 24.

It won't happen everywhere you go, but it can be shocking to some visitors to see a Wyomingite carrying a firearm openly. I sometimes spot this when I'm shopping for groceries. According to the National Rifle Association, any citizen in Wyoming over the age of 21 is permitted to openly carry a firearm in public. This law does not apply to out of state residents, a permit is required for anyone coming from another state to carry a firearm.

The use of firearms is not permitted in most tourist destinations such as state parks, campgrounds, recreational grounds, historic landmarks, or historic sites.

Wyoming is very proud of its strong stance on the 2nd Amendment of the United States Constitution and more than 60% of Wyoming residents own firearms. The state is also actively wooing manufacturers in the firearms arena to move to the state as a haven from other areas with stricter gun laws. If you feel strongly opposed to this issue, you may want to ask questions to locals about the topic, but refrain from outwardly arguing or passing judgment. Consider it a cultural difference and an opportunity to learn another point of view.

46. THE LICENSE PLATE NUMBERS

As you drive through Wyoming you'll notice that Wyoming license plates all have a prefix number on the left side. In 1930, the state gave each county the responsibility of vehicle registration and assigned each county with a number. The number is based on the value of the land within the county. Natrona County, number 1, presumably had the most valuable land in the state at the time, presumably because of its oil reserves. Cheyenne, the capital, is number 2, and Teton County, currently the most expensive county to own land in due to high demand for its natural beauty, is 22, out of 23 counties.

47. GET THE SOUVENIR YOU'VE ALWAYS WANTED

It's always nice to shop locally. The style in Wyoming has expanded beyond the cowboy to celebrate the laid back, outdoor, work hard, and play hard lifestyle that most Wyomingites live and enjoy. There are several brands that have been born and bred in Wyoming that embody this lifestyle. Check them out and grab a souvenir, not just because it's from Wyoming, but because you actually like it.

Go Slo Apparel is a brand celebrating the slower pace of life in the mountain west. This brand is based in Sheridan and sells t-shirts, sweatshirts, hats, jewelry, and original art with Wyoming, Colorado, and Montana themes.

alexis drake sells enviable higher-end leather handbags from her studio and shop in Cheyenne. She also sells jewelry, some with subtle Wyoming bison and cowgirl themes.

Surf Wyoming, also based in Sheridan, was the first Wyoming themed lifestyle brand. Beyond the popular and ruggedly stylish shirts and hats, they sell outdoor gear and other unique gift-y items.

Stio, based in Jackson Hole, retails the whole gamut of a well made outdoor apparel brand with sporty outerwear, layering items, and casual clothes for kids, women, and men.

These brands are available in retailers throughout the state, but if you were too busy to shop or don't have room in your luggage, you can find them all online

48. SMALL TOWN WITH LONG ROADS

With 563,000 residents among 62+ million acres, there's one resident per every 111 acres. Wyoming has the smallest population of any state in the country. The reality is most of the residents are clustered in several cities, but people are also scattered in the rural areas throughout the state. Locals say Wyoming is a "small town with long roads." The best advice I ever received about Wyoming is to never say a bad word about anyone (of course you wouldn't anyway because you're a nice person). There's a good chance that someone might be the cousin, aunt, or best friend of the waitress you considered rude or the cashier that did not give you the correct change. Wyoming is a close-knit community where everyone knows everybody.

49. THINGS YOU'LL OVERHEAR

Wyomingite is the correct term for a person from Wyoming.

Cowpoke is an informal name for a cowboy. When cheering for the Wyoming Cowboys, we say "Go Pokes!"

Steamboat In Wyoming you'll often see an image of a bucking horse with a cowboy rider. This horse is Steamboat, a real horse with a history of being the best bucking bronc in history. Steamboat has become a symbol of the University of Wyoming and is also seen throughout the state as a symbol of Wyoming's cowboy culture.

Bison The large, bearded, and humpbacked animal that you may encounter in Yellowstone National Park is not a buffalo and should be called a bison.

Cowboy up Quit whining, get it done.

50. PROFESSIONAL SPORTS: HOW WE SURVIVE WITHOUT THEM

Wyoming has two professional sports teams, but they are not to be missed: the Cheyenne Stampede and Yellowstone Quake, from Cody. Both are junior hockey teams that provide exciting evenings of competition. Junior hockey is often rougher, with more physical interaction between opponents, than the National Hockey League (NHL). It may be an opportunity to see the next NHL star speed across the ice.

Most people in Wyoming support and cheer for the professional teams in Colorado, particularly the Denver Broncos and the Colorado Rockies. There is true team spirit for these western teams and always strong following for the University of Wyoming Cowboys.

SPECIAL EVENTS

The Chugwater Chilli Cook-off is always the third Saturday of June in the town of Chugwater. An outdoor event with a salsa and chili competition with competitors from near and far. There is live music, food, and trinket vendors and amazing chili that participants work for years to perfect. If you miss the event, Chugwater Chilli seasoning is available year-round at tourist shops throughout the state.

Warning: The gas station in Chugwater is permanently closed, but some GPSs and maps have not been updated with this information. Fill up the car before you arrive.

Wyoming Brewers Fest is in Cheyenne, WY in June each year showcases beers from around the state. There is one fee for all you can sample of Wyoming brewed beers. The event is only for adults 21 and not accessible for anyone underage. If you're traveling with kids you may have to skip this one.

QuickDraw Art Sale is an annual event in Jackson, WY that has drawn crowds for 20 years. According to the Jackson Hole Chamber of Commerce this event, occurring at the first sign of fall in September, artists, armed with only sketches and ideas, meet in the Town Square and have 90 minutes to create their art. Visitors are welcome to wander throughout the square watching the artists at work. After the work is completed, there is a live auction and an afternoon of arts festivities.

In August, join the City of Casper for the 5150 Festival, named for the city's elevation. It is a community event downtown with live music, food, and local beer.

Sheridan hosts some unique events throughout the year including the Bighorn Rush Sled Dog Challenge in late December. This event was created to promote dog sledding. Bring your warmest layers and enjoy this one of a kind experience.

HISPANIC CULTURE

Wyoming has a strong and deep-rooted Hispanic culture that cannot be ignored. Wyoming is 10% Hispanic and in certain areas, the ratio of Hispanic/Latinos is much higher and growing. Hispanic settlers have been in Wyoming as long as European settlers, working on the railroad and the other industries that cropped up as a result of the expansion. Today the Hispanic culture is thriving. There are a few events in the state that honor the history and modern Hispanic culture in the State.

Cheyenne Hispanic Festival is held over a weekend each summer and features dance, music, art, and food from local Hispanic artists and artisans.

Fiesta Day at Cheyenne Frontier Days is a day dedicated to the history of the Latino culture in Wyoming.

Rawlins Latino Fest is a day-long event celebrating the rich Latino culture in Rawlins.

Most cities in the state hold at least one Dia de Los Muertos event, a traditional Mexican holiday honoring families and friends who have passed. It was not until attending a Dia de Los Muertos event that I learned about the Hispanic history of the state.

TOP 10 SONGS TO LISTEN TO ON YOUR WYOMING ROAD TRIP

1. Whatcha Gonna Do With A Cowboy-Chris LeDoux (Wyoming rodeo champ and country musician) featuring Garth Brooks
2. I Can Still Make Cheyenne by George Straight
3. Vedauwoo by Lowland Hum
4. Don't Fence Me In performed by the Okee Dokee Brothers (there are many versions of this song, but this is a favorite).
5. Song of Wyoming by John Denver
6. Wyoming is for Lovers by The Patti Fiasco, a popular Wyoming band
7. Sweetwater by Sycamore Treezy, a Wyoming rapper
8. Bosler by Jalan Crossland
9. Wyoming Wind performed by Caitlin Canty
10. Rodeo Cold Beer-Chancey Williams and the Younger Brothers Band, a popular Wyoming based country band

PACKING AND PLANNING TIPS

A Week before Leaving

- Arrange for someone to take care of pets and water plants.

- Email and Print important Documents.

- Get Visa and vaccines if needed.

- Check for travel warnings.

- Stop mail and newspaper.

- Notify Credit Card companies where you are going.

- Passports and photo identification is up to date.

- Pay bills.

- Copy important items and download travel Apps.

- Start collecting small bills for tips.

- Have post office hold mail while you are away.

- Check weather for the week.

- Car inspected, oil is changed, and tires have the correct pressure.

- Check airline luggage restrictions.

- Download Apps needed for your trip.

Right Before Leaving

- Contact bank and credit cards to tell them your location.

- Clean out refrigerator.

- Empty garbage cans.

- Lock windows.

- Make sure you have the proper identification with you.

- Bring cash for tips.

- Remember travel documents.

- Lock door behind you.

- Remember wallet.

- Unplug items in house and pack chargers.

- Change your thermostat settings.

- Charge electronics, and prepare camera memory cards.

READ OTHER
GREATER THAN A TOURIST
BOOKS

Greater Than a Tourist- Geneva Switzerland: 50 Travel Tips from a Local by Amalia Kartika

Greater Than a Tourist- St. Croix US Birgin Islands USA: 50 Travel Tips from a Local by Tracy Birdsall

Greater Than a Tourist- San Juan Puerto Rico: 50 Travel Tips from a Local by Melissa Tait

Greater Than a Tourist – Lake George Area New York USA: 50 Travel Tips from a Local by Janine Hirschklau

Greater Than a Tourist – Monterey California United States: 50 Travel Tips from a Local by Katie Begley

Greater Than a Tourist – Chanai Crete Greece: 50 Travel Tips from a Local by Dimitra Papagrigoraki

Greater Than a Tourist – The Garden Route Western Cape Province South Africa: 50 Travel Tips from a Local by Li-Anne McGregor van Aardt

Greater Than a Tourist – Sevilla Andalusia Spain: 50 Travel Tips from a Local by Gabi Gazon

Children's Book: *Charlie the Cavalier Travels the World* by Lisa Rusczyk Ed. D.

> TOURIST

Follow us on Instagram for beautiful travel images:
http://Instagram.com/GreaterThanATourist

Follow *Greater Than a Tourist* on Amazon.

>Tourist Podcast

>T Website

>T Youtube

>T Facebook

>T Goodreads

>T Amazon

>T Mailing List

>T Pinterest

>T Instagram

>T Twitter

>T SoundCloud

>T LinkedIn

>T Map

> TOURIST

At *Greater Than a Tourist*, we love to share travel tips with you. How did we do? What guidance do you have for how we can give you better advice for your next trip? Please send your feedback to GreaterThanaTourist@gmail.com as we continue to improve the series. We appreciate your constructive feedback. Thank you.

METRIC CONVERSIONS

TEMPERATURE

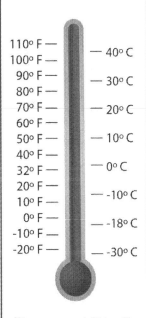

110° F — — 40° C
100° F —
90° F — — 30° C
80° F —
70° F — — 20° C
60° F —
50° F — — 10° C
40° F —
32° F — — 0° C
20° F —
10° F — — -10° C
0° F —
-10° F — — -18° C
-20° F — — -30° C

To convert F to C:

Subtract 32, and then multiply by 5/9 or .5555.

To Convert C to F:
Multiply by 1.8 and then add 32.

32F = 0C

LIQUID VOLUME

To Convert:.................Multiply by
U.S. Gallons to Liters................ 3.8
U.S. Liters to Gallons 26
Imperial Gallons to U.S. Gallons 1.2
Imperial Gallons to Liters...... 4.55
Liters to Imperial Gallons 22
1 Liter = .26 U.S. Gallon
1 U.S. Gallon = 3.8 Liters

DISTANCE

To convert ....Multiply by
Inches to Centimeters 2.54
Centimeters to Inches 39
Feet to Meters...................... .3
Meters to Feet 3.28
Yards to Meters 91
Meters to Yards 1.09
Miles to Kilometers 1.61
Kilometers to Miles............ .62
1 Mile = 1.6 km
1 km = .62 Miles

WEIGHT

1 Ounce = .28 Grams
1 Pound = .4555 Kilograms
1 Gram = .04 Ounce
1 Kilogram = 2.2 Pounds

TRAVEL QUESTIONS

- Do you bring presents home to family or friends after a vacation?

- Do you get motion sick?

- Do you have a favorite billboard?

- Do you know what to do if there is a flat tire?

- Do you like a sun roof open?

- Do you like to eat in the car?

- Do you like to wear sun glasses in the car?

- Do you like toppings on your ice cream?

- Do you use public bathrooms?

- Did you bring a cell phone and does it have power?

- Do you have a form of identification with you?

- Have you ever been pulled over by a cop?

- Have you ever given money to a stranger on a road trip?

- Have you ever taken a road trip with animals?

- Have you ever gone on a vacation alone?

- Have you ever run out of gas?

- If you could move to any place in the world, where would it be?

- If you could travel anywhere in the world, where would you travel?

- If you could travel in any vehicle, which one would it be?

- If you had three things to wish for from a magic genie, what would they be?

- If you have a driver's license, how many times did it take you to pass the test?

- What are you the most afraid of on vacation?

- What do you want to get away from the most when you are on vacation?

- What foods smell bad to you?

- What item do you bring on ever trip with you away from home?

- What makes you sleepy?

- What song would you love to hear on the radio when you're cruising on the highway?

- What travel job would you want the least?

- What will you miss most while you are away from home?

- What is something you always wanted to try?

- What is the best road side attraction that you ever saw?

- What is the farthest distance you ever biked?

- What is the farthest distance you ever walked?

- What is the weirdest thing you needed to buy while on vacation?

- What is your favorite candy?

- What is your favorite color car?

- What is your favorite family vacation?

- What is your favorite food?

- What is your favorite gas station drink or food?

- What is your favorite license plate design?

- What is your favorite restaurant?

- What is your favorite smell?

- What is your favorite song?

- What is your favorite sound that nature makes?

- What is your favorite thing to bring home from a vacation?

- What is your favorite vacation with friends?

- What is your favorite way to relax?

- Where is the farthest place you ever traveled in a car?

- Where is the farthest place you ever went North, South, East and West?

- Where is your favorite place in the world?

- Who is your favorite singer?

- Who taught you how to drive?

- Who will you miss the most while you are away?

- Who if the first person you will contact when you get to your destination?

- Who brought you on your first vacation?

- Who likes to travel the most in your life?

- Would you rather be hot or cold?

- Would you rather drive above, below, or at the speed limited?

- Would you rather drive on a highway or a back road?

- Would you rather go on a train or a boat?

- Would you rather go to the beach or the woods?

TRAVEL BUCKET LIST

1.

2.

3.

4.

5.

6.

7.

8.

9.

10.

NOTES

Printed in Great Britain
by Amazon

66992690R00061